GEORGE
BENSON
Biography

American Guitarist, Songwriter, And One of The Highest-Paid Musicians in The World

MAURICE PENCE

TABLE OF CONTENTS

INTRODUCTION

In the vibrant tapestry of musical history, there are those rare individuals who, from a tender age, possess an innate talent that sets them apart.

Such is the case with George Benson, a music legend whose journey through the world of music began at the tender age of seventeen.

It was during this formative period that Benson, driven by an insatiable passion for rhythm and blues, fearlessly embarked on a path that would forever shape his destiny.

With a vision in his heart and a guitar in his hands, Benson fearlessly assembled a five-piece R&B ensemble, a harmonious collective that would serve as the vessel for his artistic expression.

As the group's leader, he not only lent his soulful voice to their melodic tapestry but also wielded his rhythmic guitar with an effortless finesse that captivated all who had the privilege of witnessing his virtuosity.

It was during this pivotal time that an extraordinary opportunity presented itself, forever altering the course of his musical destiny.

Benson found himself prepared to start a remarkable chapter in his developing career thanks to an invitation from none other than the esteemed Jack McDuff, a renowned organist.

As the electric guitar became his instrument of choice within McDuff's organ trio, the stage was set for Benson to make his mark and leave an indelible imprint on the annals of music history.

Little did he know, this would be the first significant break that would set the wheels of his musical odyssey into motion.

This book revolves around a remarkable individual who, after years of performing and recording alongside the esteemed McDuff, made the audacious decision to embark on a journey of his own.

In the year 1965, he bid farewell to the band that had become his musical home, setting forth to establish his own quartets and assuming the leadership role.

It was during this fateful year that a young prodigy emerged from the shadows, ready to make his indelible mark on the world of music.

With great anticipation and a sense of destiny, Benson unveiled his inaugural masterpiece, an album that would come to be known as "Benson Burner."

This groundbreaking opus would not only showcase his extraordinary talent as a leader but also serve as a testament to his boundless creativity.

While his vocals may not have garnered the same acclaim as those of his peers, it was his magnificently blistering guitar solos that set him apart.

With each stroke of the strings, he wove a tapestry of sound that left audiences spellbound, their hearts racing to keep up with the rhythm of his fingers.

As whispers of his talent spread through the jazz community, his reputation as an up-and-coming force to be reckoned with grew.

Join us as we delve into the captivating tale of a musician who dared to break free and chart his own musical odyssey.

Chapter 1

EARLY LIFE

Who is George Benson?

George Benson is able to successfully gather admirers in both the realm of pop music and the world of jazz. He is recognized for his warm singing voice, which has been included on many albums that have been financially successful.

He first gained prominence in the music business as a young and inventive jazz guitarist. After spending a significant portion of his career producing and performing largely pop music, he picked up playing classic jazz again.

Benson's singing career seems to have begun not long after he was able to communicate verbally. In 1947, when he was just four years old, he won a singing contest and sang on the radio as "Little Georgie Benson."

After that, he started singing in bars and on the street, where a talent scout first saw him at the age of eleven.

His debut track, an R&B song called "She Makes Me Mad," was released on the RCA label as a result of this discovery. Benson claims jazz great Eddie Jefferson as an early influence on his voice, and Jefferson was also an influence on his playing.

George Benson shared his thoughts with Down Beat writer Lois Gilbert, where he expressed his feeling that Eddie Jefferson was one of the greatest jazz singers the world had known. He was to him the Bebop King.

His interest in jazz was piqued by listening to records of influential musicians like saxophonist Charlie Parker and guitarist Grant Green.

George Benson is a performer on the guitar, vocals, and composition. He has worked as a sideman and led his own quartets as a guitarist and singer since 1965.

More so, George Benson was a recording artist with Columbia Records from 1965 to

1968. He collaborated with producer Creed Taylor, first at A&M Records and then at Taylor's CTI label, from 1968 to 1972.

He also worked as a recording artist with Warner Bros. Records in 1976.

Birth And Upbringing in Pittsburgh, Pennsylvania

On March 22, 1943, George Benson was born in the city of Pittsburgh, in the state of Pennsylvania. He spent his childhood in Pittsburgh's Hill District, where he later dropped out of Connelley High School, which has since closed its doors.

Benson displayed his skill at an early age, winning a singing contest when he was just four years old and going on to have a brief career as a child radio artist under the moniker "Little Georgie Benson."

At the age of eight, he began his career as a vocalist and began singing in nightclubs. During this time, he also learned how to dance and play the ukulele.

After he had recorded four sides for the X Records subsidiary of RCA Victor in the middle of the 1950s, his stepfather encouraged him to focus on developing his musical skills and built a guitar for him.

Benson started to focus all of his attention solely on the guitar when he was in his late teens, and at the age of 17, he established his own rock band.

GEORGE BENSON'S BIOGRAPHY

His introduction to the music of jazz musicians like Charlie Christian, Grant Green, and Wes Montgomery on record, as well as the saxophonist Charlie Parker, was the spark that ignited his interest in the genre.

Musical Beginnings

The great guitarist Wes Montgomery served as a model for Benson's career as a younger artist, and his influence can be seen in George Benson's guitar playing style, particularly his use of octave playing and his smooth tone.

Creed Taylor, who first helped Montgomery transition from jazz performing to pop success and later did the same for Benson, was their producer.

Worthy of note is that both Benson and Montgomery worked for Creed Taylor. Benson first collaborated with Taylor when the two were employed at A&M Records.

In 1970, Benson joined Taylor at his newly founded CTI label. Despite the fact that Benson continued to play guitar, Taylor attempted to highlight his singing by providing an orchestral background for his voice.

Nevertheless, Benson continued to record jazz that received widespread acclaim, notably on his 1971 album Beyond the Blue Horizon.

Chapter 2

RISE TO FAME

Professional Journey

Benson started off his professional life as a guitarist and vocalist, playing in various rhythm-and-blues and rock bands in the corner pubs of his hometown of Pittsburgh.

He worked as an apprentice for the organist "Brother" Jack McDuff in the early 1960s, and by the time he was 21, he had already released his first album as a leader.

In 1964, he made his first album, which was titled The New Boss Guitar, and McDuff played the organ on it.

19

Early Performances and Collaborations with Notable Artists

At the age of seventeen, Benson formed a five-piece R&B ensemble in which he sang and played rhythm guitar as the group's leader.

Benson had his first significant break in the music industry in 1961 when he was invited to become an electric guitarist in Jack McDuff's organ trio.

He continued to perform and record with McDuff until 1965. Following a period of four years of performing and recording with McDuff, Benson struck out on his own and relocated to New York City, which at the time was widely regarded as the jazz center of the world.

After he parted ways with the band, he formed his own quartet and took the helm. He made the acquaintance of Wes Montgomery, a guitarist, as well as John Hammond, a producer and executive at Columbia Records, when he was in New York.

It was Montgomery, one of jazz's most creative guitarists, who first encountered Benson. Montgomery complimented the young guitarist and encouraged him to continue his excellent work.

Benson would establish his own unique playing style, and Montgomery proved to be the most significant influence on Benson's style.

Interestingly, George Benson was one of the most significant talents that Hammond unearthed and brought to the public's attention in the year 1965.

The ever-expanding list of Benson's sideman credentials, which included work with musicians like Herbie Hancock, Freddie Hubbard, and Miles Davis, left him feeling rather pleased.

In addition, George Benson has performed as a sideman for jazz greats such as Ron Carter, Billy Cobham, and Lee Morgan.

Additionally, he was a participant in his own organization. The year 1967 saw the

22

release of Benson's first album as a leader, titled Benson Burner.

His vocals were deemed to be mediocre; nonetheless, his magnificently blistering guitar solos were praised as the work of an up-and-coming jazz musician.

Signing With Columbia Records

Benson was signed to Columbia Records by Hammond in 1965, and he would go on to record three albums for the label. On his first record, titled It's Uptown, Lonnie Smith played the organ while Ronnie Cuber played the baritone saxophone.

This record, as well as his second album, Benson Burner, were both produced by

Hammond and were in the major bop-influenced vein of jazz music of the time.

Hammond's first album was titled Benson. The jazz world reacted favorably to the young guitarist's performance as a result of this attention.

After releasing his first two albums, Benson released The George Benson Cookbook the following year, in 1966. This album also included Lonnie Smith and Ronnie Cuber.

He was able to find time to concentrate on other projects in addition to making records with Hammond. One of these side projects was Benson's collaboration with Miles Davis in the middle of the 1960s.

Benson was enlisted by Davis to provide his talents for the recording of Miles in the Sky, which was released by Columbia in 1967.

On the song "Paraphernalia," he was featured on guitar. Benson, on the other hand, was looking for larger public attention and switched labels many times in the process.

Chapter 3

HIS SWITCH TO A&M AND CTI RECORDINGS

After signing with Verve in 1967 and recording three albums for them, he moved on to A&M in 1968, where he worked on many projects, one of which was a cover of The Beatles' album Abbey Road titled The Other Side of Abbey Road, which was released the following year.

Creed Taylor, a jazz producer who had collaborated with Montgomery, one of Benson's teachers, was a significant source of inspiration for George Benson.

Taylor started recording Benson with different huge ensembles on the A&M label between the years 1968 and 1969, and he recorded big groups and all-star combinations for the CTI label between the years 1971 and 1976.

Montgomery had passed away in June 1968. Benson became a guitar superstar in the jazz world as a result of the A&M and CTI recordings.

However, the vocal tracks he recorded for the albums reawakened his interest in singing, and his decision to place a focus on vocals would prove to be an essential component of his subsequent achievements.

Warner Bros.

Benson was unhappy with the amount of liberty he was given under Taylor's leadership, so he made yet another shift in record labels towards the end of 1975 when he inked a deal with Warner Bros.

This move was significant since it paved the path for his entry into the mainstream market. Benson, despite his early success, wanted to integrate his singing and playing of the guitar into a single career.

Tommy LiPuma, a music producer, was able to combine his skills, which resulted in the release of Breezin', which was the first jazz album to achieve platinum sales.

This groundbreaking album, which was released in 1976, was the first of many that George Benson would make for Warner Bros.

The record contained a song with a pop-oriented vocal track by Leon Russell titled "This Masquerade," which featured the guitarist scatting along with his guitar solo break.

The album was able to attain the same place on the pop charts thanks to the success of a single track that not only won a Grammy Award for Record of the Year but also topped the charts for jazz and R&B music.

Furthermore, the record was honored with three Grammy Awards and went on to become the all-time leader in sales for a jazz album.

The instrumental title track from Breezin' was first broadcast on jazz radio, and George Benson's characteristic sound—scat singing along with his guitar and doubling it at the interval of an octave—was presented for the first time.

Benson developed a unique connection and rapport with his guitar as a result of his scat singing. Benson said in an interview with Guitar Player magazine that when he picks up the guitar, it's an extension of who he is.

His vocals were first met with disapproval in the recording studio as he attempted to experiment with the sound of his new instrument.

Benson shared his experience, saying, "*When I initially took my guitar into the recording studio, the whole audience booed me.*"

Nobody thought that anything like that could actually happen. All of that changed the moment he became acquainted with Tommy LiPuma.

It was LiPuma's response that Benson will always remember: "*Sure, let's go with some vocals and see where we get.*" And subsequently, a lot of positive changes occurred.

32

Following the critical and financial acclaim that Breezin' received, Benson went on to release a string of albums that would primarily feature his vocals and enjoy success in the marketplace.

Chapter 4

MUSICAL EVOLUTION

Experimentation With Different Genres and Sounds

When George Benson had a recording career in the late 1970s, releasing albums for both the Warner Brothers and CTI labels, his records gravitated more toward the pop genre.

Thus, he began to place more emphasis on his vocals than on his guitar skills. Benson started to come under fire from purists of the jazz genre, who believed that he had sold out his early artistic endeavors in favor of commercial success.

Benson said, "*I guess that's the biggest crime I've committed as far as jazz lovers go. It is not always to their liking to see you perform in front of the entire audience,*" he said with a sense of humor.

George Benson has always made it a point to let his experience do the talking whenever possible. According to him, people grow as a result of what they learn.

Despite this criticism, Benson was able to achieve significant commercial success, notably with his album "Weekend in L.A." from 1978.

This album includes the live version of "On Broadway," which won the Grammy Award for Best Contemporary Instrumental Performance.

The successful album peaked at number one on the charts for both jazz and R&B, as well as at number five on the list for overall album sales in the United States.

The Return with A Breakthrough Album In 1980

George Benson returned in 1980 with another breakthrough album titled Give Me the Night, which included the single title tune.

It reached its highest position on the pop chart in the United States at number four. The album was the climax of a succession of successful albums in an R&B-flavored pop genre, and Quincy Jones served as the producer of the record.

At this point in time, Benson's guitar had been consigned to the background, and the spotlight had been placed on his vocals as well as more commercially viable formulae.

This was even more clear in Benson's smash track "Turn Your Love Around," which topped the R&B chart and almost topped the pop chart in the United States, reaching number five in 1981.

Benson maintained his recording career throughout the 1980s, releasing a string of songs that were only moderately successful commercially, including "Lady Love Me

(One More Time)" in 1983 and "20/20" in 1984.

Benson continued to face criticism for the commercialization of his art, despite the fact that his guitar work was becoming progressively less prominent in his albums.

In his review of Benson's album "In Your Eyes," which was released in 1983, Richard S. Ginell of the All-Music Guide to Jazz made the following observation: "*The guitar time on Benson's recordings is so little at this stage that finding it is like digging for lost treasure for jazz enthusiasts.*"

Memorable Albums and Live Performances

After getting his start in the recording industry at a young age, Benson collaborated with a number of well-known jazz musicians in the 1960s, including Jack McDuff and Miles Davis, among others.

His breakout hit came in the 1970s with his 1976 record Breezin', which contained the title tune and "This Masquerade."

It was during this period that he also started doing live performances. Another big album, Give Me the Night, was released in 1980, and a smash single, "Turn Your Love Around," was released in 1981.

After that, a slew of more popular albums and singles followed. He has been awarded

40

a great number of accolades, including eight Grammys, and has had multiple albums certified gold and platinum.

Benson has maintained a career as one of the most active performers in the entertainment industry, recording new albums and continuing to give live performances throughout the 1980s, 1990s, and 2000s.

The work that Benson did as a jazz guitarist is what brought him the greatest fame; nevertheless, he is also a pop, R&B, and soul vocalist as well as a composer.

Chapter 5

MUSICAL STYLE, INNOVATIONS, AND CRITICISMS

Return To Jazz

The critical reception that Benson received throughout the 1970s and early 1980s, despite his economic success, was largely due to the fact that he had almost abandoned conventional jazz.

The fact that he could not live up to his early potential as a jazz guitarist was a source of disappointment for purists of the genre.

Although he had dabbled in playing jazz guitar in the past, as evidenced by his performance with Benny Goodman on public

43

television's Soundstage Tribute to John Hammond, he did not devote an entire album to his jazz playing until 1989.

In 1989, Benson shifted his focus from pop to jazz with a beautiful album of standards titled Tenderly, which he recorded with the famed jazz pianists McCoy Tyner, Lenny Castro, and Ron Carter.

Over the course of the summer of 1989, Benson also went on tour with the McCoy Tyner Trio. He said the following in Down Beat on his desire to return to playing jazz guitar: "*With Tenderly, I very much felt I was reestablishing my jazz credentials, and, although it took audiences a little while to get used to it, the response was eventually overwhelming."*

He made that statement in reference to his decision to return to playing jazz guitar.

Benson was encouraged to attempt a jazz album with the Count Basie Orchestra (CBO) by the positive reception he received for his jazz skills.

The record that they worked on together, titled Big Boss Band, was released in 1990 and garnered positive reviews.

At the last minute, Ella Fitzgerald was unable to perform at the North Sea Jazz Festival in the same year, so Benson stood in for her and performed three songs with the CBO.

He told the reporter for Down Beat, Michael Bourne, "*We had no rehearsal except for what we'd done in the studio, but the great vibe was still there.*"

Benson's return to jazz was a display of his flexibility as a musician, with his ability to perform with a broad variety of arrangements, from tiny ensembles to large bands, with a string section, with hard bop, and with Latin-inflected choices.

His return to the jazz genre served as an exhibition of his ability to perform with a broad array of different arrangements.

As he continued to perform in several concert venues and consolidated his fame during the 1990s, he was able to maintain a healthy equilibrium between the two musical subgenres because of the success he had gained in both the jazz and pop music worlds.

Benson collaborated with Jack McDuff once again in 1992, this time performing on the latter's album titled Color Me Blue.

Introduction Of Scat Singing to His Performances

Scat singing a line that is similar to the tune that he plays on the guitar has been Benson's signature, and it has garnered him the affection of music lovers as well as music journalists.

In most cases, he sings in perfect harmony with his guitar playing; nevertheless, on occasion, his singing will be either an octave higher or lower than his playing.

Even less often, you'll hear him singing along with his guitar. Benson once explained that his guitar can do things that his voice can't.

When he's simply doing the vocal, it may soar, which causes his voice to attempt to follow it, and as a result, Benson winds up singing in octaves that his voice is unable to achieve on its own.

His voice keeps going even though he is trying to play the guitar at the same time. It accompanies the guitar all the way up and down the scale, and it does it continuously.

Sometimes it feels like he does not even have an idea how he's capable of getting that much range.

Criticism

Benson's efforts to combine the positions of guitarist and singer, jazz pioneer, and commercial success have, on occasion, led to criticism of his lack of devotion to pure jazz.

This criticism has periodically led to Benson's retirement from the music industry. However, his efforts in the late 1980s to achieve his early potential as a jazz musician have resulted in the development of his pop following among jazz fans.

This was the outcome of his attempts to fulfill his early promise as a jazz performer. Benson explored going on a global tour with the Count Basie Orchestra and worked on a record with Jon Hendricks, Al Jarreau, and Bobby McFerrin during the early 1990s.

These events were indicative of the continuation of this growth, which was evident throughout the decade.

Chapter 6

JAZZ-ORIENTED GRP LABEL

After recording his album Love Remembers in 1993 for Warner Bros., he later parted ways with the company and signed with the jazz-oriented GRP label in 1996, at which time he released the album That's Right.

In the same year, Benson was recognized at the Mellon Jazz Festival in Pittsburgh, which was celebrating its 10th year.

Other jazz greats who performed at the festival that year included saxophonist Joe Lovano, Dizzy Gillespie/Charlie Parker sideman Jimmy Heath, and avant-garde composer John Zorn.

51

Benson made his way back into the recording studio in 1998 to work on the smooth jazz album Standing Together.

His Latter Significant Recordings and Collaboration With Al Jarreau

His latter significant recordings include the albums "Absolute Benson" (released in 2000), "All Blues" (released in 2001), and "Irreplaceable" (released in 2004).

In 2006, Benson and jazz performer and longtime friend Al Jarreau collaborated on the recording of Givin' It Up, which was released by Concord Records in October of the same year.

Benson and Jarreau were two threads in the legendary 1970s tapestry that was the Warner Brothers record company.

They left an unmistakable stamp on the history of music with their performances, which echoed through the halls of this prestigious establishment.

In the heart of Los Angeles, at the Ambassador Hotel, fate brought together two extraordinary individuals. Benson and Jarreau adorned the stage while the stars above them glistened, their songs entwining in a dance of musical splendor.

Their vocals soared in the acoustics of this sacred space, mesmerizing the rapt crowd. There was a palpable electric sensation in the room as the symbiotic bond between these two lights went beyond simple cooperation.

Their time together at the Warner Brothers label formed a connection that would follow them throughout their careers as artists.

Through the passage of time, their collaboration at the Ambassador Hotel has become a shining example of the transcendent craftsmanship that may occur when two outstanding talents come together.

This meant that they were no strangers to one another. After Benson had already signed with Concord, Jarreau started talking with record executives, which is

54

when this new coupling was conceived of and eventually put into motion.

Jarreau recounted an encounter where he engaged in a conversation with Concord. During this interaction, he maintained a focused and attentive demeanor.

Subsequently, one of the executives summoned both Jarreau and George to their office and posed the question, "What are your thoughts on collaborating to produce a record?"

Both of them exchanged glances and then murmured in unison, "Let's go!" Before the record was ever officially released, the numerous Grammy Award winners went on tour in the United States, South Africa, Australia, and New Zealand to promote it.

Jarreau said that the collaboration is an example of a lot of what he and George typically do, which is pop and R&B within a jazz context.

The album garnered positive reviews from music journalists and was shortlisted for three Grammy Awards, ultimately taking home two of them.

Benson and Jarreau's performance in Pittsburgh's Heinz Hall on June 19, 2007, marked the return of the Hill District native, who had previously played there with Jarreau for a Mellon Jazz event.

His Personal Misfortunes

Benson's life has been marred by personal sorrow despite all of the success he has achieved. Three of their seven kids have passed away: one due to renal failure, one due to a death that occurred in the infant's cradle, and one due to gunshot wounds sustained as a result of a bar brawl.

Mohammed Al Fayed approached him in 1998 and requested that he compose a song in memory of his son, Dodi, who had been killed in a car accident in Paris in 1997 together with his close friend Princess Diana of England.

The song was to be performed in Dodi's honor. Benson told his wife about the song

57

and the impact it had on him emotionally, and they both listened to it together.

It was reported that Benson said something like, "*During the writing, I asked my wife to come listen to what I had written. However, after I reached a certain point, it became impossible for me to continue.*

"*My mouth was quivering uncontrollably. I was dwelling on my personal misfortunes and found that I was unable to move on from them. It gave me the creeps all the way down my spine,*" says Benson.

He has been able to keep going forward despite all that has happened to him, and he attributes his faith and his success to his decision to become a Jehovah's Witness.

The musician, who was born in Pittsburgh, was selected as one of the National Endowment for the Arts Jazz Masters for 2009 and was celebrated at Jazz at Lincoln Center in New York City on October 17, 2008.

Benson maintains a hectic schedule by continually creating new songs and playing over one hundred performances every year while traveling the globe.

He is presently leading a solitary life in Arizona and is back in the studio creating a new album with a superb cast of musicians, which includes keyboardist/vocalist David Paich of the rock/pop band Toto and guitarist/vocalist Steve Lukather of the band.

Chapter 7

PERSONAL LIFE

George Benson's Wife

George Benson met Johnnie, the woman he would go on to spend the next decades of his life with, in the early phases of his professional life.

The American jazz singer, who is now 80 years old, has been married to Johnnie for a long time. The first day of the year 1965 marked the beginning of their romantic relationship.

Collectively, they proceeded to birth a total of seven male offspring.

When it comes to his romantic relationships, George Benson maintains a level of privacy that is admirable.

George Benson's Dating Compatibility

Aries, the sign that George Benson was born in, is governed by the planet Mars. There are two more fire signs that are most romantically compatible with Aries: Leo and Aquarius.

This zodiac sign enjoys the thrill of the chase and has a propensity to rush into love rapidly, but just as swiftly, they tend to rush out of love just as soon.

Cancer and Capricorn are the signs that are least compatible with Pisces when it comes to dating. The goat is George's animal sign, according to the zodiac.

The Goat is the eighth animal in the Zodiac and is known for being creative, melancholy, and compassionate.

According to the laws of the Chinese zodiac for compatibility, the Horse, Pig, and Rabbit signs are those with whom the Goat sign has the most potential for love and platonic relationships.

When selecting a spouse, however, you should steer clear of those whose horoscopes include the ox, rat, or dog.

George Benson Is the Highest-Paid Guitarist in The World.

In the year 2020, it seemed as if the phenomenal career of the musician was coming to an end. Instantaneously, he regained his dominant position.

The guitarist has had challenging years, but at least he can take solace in the fact that he has millions of dollars to his name.

According to a survey published by People With Money, George Benson, who is now 80 years old, is the highest-paid guitarist in the world.

Between May 2022 and May 2023, he made an astounding $96 million, giving him a lead of about $60 million over his nearest competitor.

His Net Worth

According to People With Money's factors, it is believed that the musician and vocalist from the United States has a net worth of $275 million.

When preparing this list on an annual basis, the magazine takes into consideration a number of different aspects, including upfront salary, profit share, residuals, endorsements, and advertising work.

George Benson amassed his wealth via shrewd stock investments, extensive property holdings, and lucrative endorsement partnerships with CoverGirl cosmetics, among other things.

In addition, he is the owner of a football team known as the "Pittsburgh Angels," a chain of restaurants known as "Fat Benson Burger," and his very own line of vodka known as "Pure Wonderbenson," which is sold in the United States.

Benson is currently attempting to break into the junior market with a successful fragrance known as "With Love from George" as well as a clothing line titled "George Benson Seduction."

The ranking is crucial for many George fans, as they have been waiting for what feels like an eternity for their favorite musician to make his triumphant comeback to the golden days of his career.

Chapter 8

GEORGE BENSON'S 10 BEST SONGS

Love X Love

This song was written and recorded by Heatwave's keyboard player, Rod Temperton, who also penned 'Thriller' for Michael Jackson.

The song was produced by the deft hands of none other than the legendary Quincy Jones. Although it was not successful in the United States, it did make it to number 10 in the UK in 1980.

Breezin'

This tune was originally an instrumental song that was created by the American vocalist Bobby Womack and recorded with the legendary Hungarian jazz guitarist Gábor Szabó.

After another five years, the smooth jazz tune achieved even more notoriety as a result of George's popular rendition of it; the latter went on to become the title track of his subsequent album.

Lady, Love Me (One More Time)

Toto vocalist David Paich and James Newton Howard, who won a Grammy

Award for his work in film scoring, collaborated on the composition of this song.

It was more successful in the United Kingdom, where it peaked at number 11 in 1983, than it was in the United States.

Turn Your Love around.

This song was composed by three of the most talented composers in the world: Steve Lukather of Toto, Bill Champlin of Chicago, and producer and guitarist Jay Graydon.

Graydon was in an unusual setting when he first had the idea for the song, but he was still sitting down when the melody came to him.

He got off the can as quickly as he could and made his way to a tape machine in order to ensure that he wouldn't forget it.

Since George Benson was going to be performing there in a few days, Graydon had four days to compose a song for him.

On Broadway

This classic was written by legendary songwriters Barry Mann and Cynthia Weil, together with Jerry Leiber and Mike Stoller. The Drifters made it their own in 1963, and it became one of their most famous songs.

Since then, it has been recorded by a great number of musicians, including George

Benson, who released his smooth jazz rendition in 1978.

A sequence from the 1979 movie All That Jazz showed dancers trying out for a musical that was similar to Chicago. The scenario included George's performance of the song, and it was utilized in the scene.

The Greatest Love of All

In 1976, George was the first artist to record this song, and it quickly rose to the top 30 on the charts in both the United Kingdom and the United States.

It was composed to serve as the primary theme of the 1977 film The Greatest, which was about boxer Muhammad Ali.

When Whitney Houston finally released her own cover of the song eight years later, she included it on her first album, where it quickly became a massive smash.

Give Me the Night

Another composition by Rod Temperton, this song was included on his album of the same name, which was released in 1980.

In addition, Patti Austin was responsible for the backup vocals that can be heard throughout the track.

It reached number 10 on the charts in both the United Kingdom and the United States, and it is widely considered to be one of the most successful disco songs of all time.

Nothing's Going to Change My Love for You.

In 1985, George had some success with this song, which was written by Masser and Gerry Goffin.

Nevertheless, it is most likely better remembered as a cover by Glenn Medeiros, who in 1988 took it to number one in the UK with his version of the song.

In Your Eyes

Michael Masser and Dan Hill, the vocalist from 'Sometimes When We Touch,' collaborated to write this heartfelt love ballad.

George Benson had yet another moderate amount of success in the UK with this song, which peaked at number 7 in 1983.

Neva Giv Up on A Good Thing.

Surprisingly, this pop hit from 1982 only reached number 14 on the charts in the UK, while it only reached number 52 in the United States.

The song is today considered one of George Benson's most iconic works since it was included on the compilation album "The George Benson Collection", which featured the artist's greatest hits.

Printed in Great Britain
by Amazon

39134602R00046